The Sex Position Playbook

69 POSITIONS FOR INCREDIBLE PLEASURE

QUIVER

Contents

INTRODUCTION	4
HOW TO USE THIS BOOK	5

THE BASICS

Missionary	7
Cowgirl	8
Spooning	11
Doggie Style	12
69	15
Reverse Cowgirl	16
Yab-Yum	19
Loving Spoons	20
Counter Service	23
Lazy Dog	24

PLEASE BE SEATED

Lazy AF	27
The Lap Dance	28
Chair Doggie	31
Best Seat in the House	32
Titanic	35

STANDING O

Stand and Deliver	36
Standing Room Only	39
I Must Have You Now	40
The Pat-Down	43
Leg Day	44
Back That Azz UP	47
The Tree House	48

TWEAKS THAT CHANGE EVERYTHING

Gender Is a Construct Missionary	51
Pressed Missionary	52
Flying V	55
CAT Power	56
Slow Jam	59
The Love Seat	60
The Bridge	63
The Windshield Wipers	64
The Snake Charmer	67
Sideways 69	68
The Humper	71
Sealed with a Twist	72

THE INTERMEDIATE LEVEL

Twister	75
Splitting of Bamboo	76
Squat Thrust Crab	79
The Mmmm	80
Saddleback	83
The Hot Seat	84
Indecent Proposal	87
The Rocking Horse	88
Supercharged 69	91
Slip 'n Slide	92
Your Table Is Ready	95
Froggie Style	96
T-Top	99
Titty F*ck	100

KINK CURIOUS

All Tied Up	103
You Shall Service Me	104
Get to Work	107
Bend Over and Take It	108
In Your Face	111
The Spanking Machine	112
Sex Doll	115

ADVANCED MODE

Face/Off	116
The Field Hand	119
The Sculpture	120
X Marks the Spot	123
The Lawn Mower	124
Opposite Day	127
The Launch Pad	128
The Pretzel	131
Have a Seat	132
The Beach Chair	135
The Hokey Pokey	136
The Rocking Chair	139
Forbidden Yoga	140
The Starter Gun	143

Introduction

You already know a few ways to get your body parts in, on, or next to each other. That's cool. Missionaries supposedly had their one position, and they still managed to get with each other plenty.

But. Adding new positions to your roster adds a little bit of magic pixie dust to your sexing. Positions can be hot and animalistic or deep and soulful. Some might hit a fun new angle or highlight one of your favorite body parts. You might uncover something new you're into or find variations on an old favorite theme.

This book works for any gender and sexuality combination you have going on. A few of them only work if there's a vulva on board, but lots of them work anally or vaginally. Augment with hands, a strap-on, or your mouth. And there's gender-neutral language throughout. We're using the terms "giver" for the person who is penetrating or giving oral sex and "receiver" for the person getting the oral sex or the penetration.

Somewhere in this book is your new favorite position, or maybe sixty-nine new favorites (go, you!). Have fun testing them out.

How to Use This Book

Use this book however you'd like! Take it on vacation, open to a random page, and voilà!, that's your plan for the night. Flip through the pages together and pick some for your sex position bucket list. Take turns picking a position and giving it a go. Create a sex positions playbook and cycle through three or four during a session. Up to you.

Some of these positions might be a hard pass for you. Totally okay. If something seems sus, go ahead and avoid it. No points deducted. Move along and do another one. If you see a promising one but think your body can't/doesn't want to bend that way—again, all good. Don't do that one. And if something doesn't feel good, go ahead and stop. This is about pleasure.

And even though these positions all have specific instructions, feel free to tweak them as you please. Try a different hip angle, switch places, or throw in some toys. With sixty-nine (nice) positions to choose from, you've got *options*.

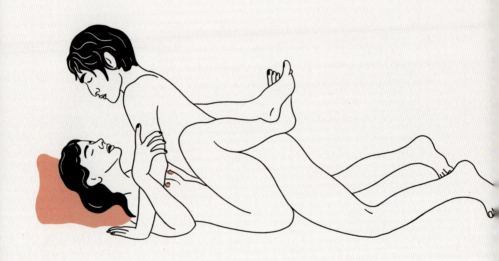

Missionary

THE STARTER SIM OF SEX POSITIONS, MISSIONARY HAS BEEN A FAVORITE POSITION PRETTY MUCH FOREVER.

HOW TO DO IT

The receiver lies on their back with their legs spread and positioned in whatever way feels comfortable. The giver lies on top of their partner with their hips between the receiver's legs, holding their weight on their elbows and forearms.

WHAT'S GOOD ABOUT IT

Lots of skin-to-skin contact and opportunities for kissing and eye gazing. It's also very adjustable—the receiver can move their legs for different angles of stimulation. Plus, everyone kind of understands what they're supposed to be doing.

MAKE IT BETTER

Missionary doesn't have to be vanilla! Trick it out with props, toys, or whatever you please.

Cowgirl

RIDE THAT HORSEY.

HOW TO DO IT

The giver lies flat on their back. The receiver gets on their knees and straddles their partner. The receiver can lean forward and rest their hands on their partner's chest or the bed if they want more leverage.

WHAT'S GOOD ABOUT IT

Cowgirl gives the person on top free rein (…) to control the speed, depth, and angle of penetration. If the person on top has a vulva, cowgirl can be more orgasmic than many other positions because they're in full control of their own stimulation.

MAKE IT BETTER

For a more dominant vibe, the person on top can hold onto their partner's wrists to pin them down.

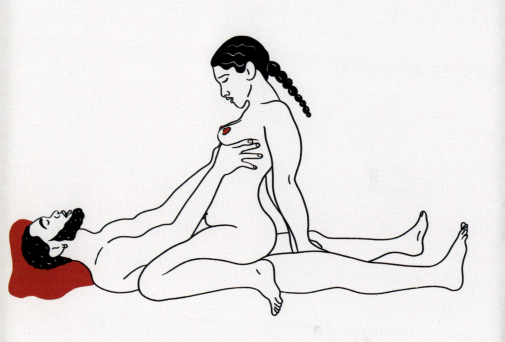

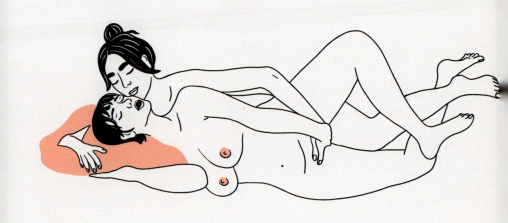

Spooning
AREN'T YOU TWO ADORABLE?

HOW TO DO IT

One person (a.k.a. the little spoon) lies on their side. The other person (the big spoon) also lies on their side behind their partner so they can wrap their arms around them and hold them close.

WHAT'S GOOD ABOUT IT

Since you're basically hugging while having sex, it's about as romantic as it gets. This position works well for leisurely morning sex or as way to end the day in each other's arms. It's also good for people with mobility issues.

MAKE IT BETTER

The big spoon can reach around to stroke the little spoon's penis/vulva with a hand or a toy.

Doggie Style

GO AT IT LIKE A COUPLE OF ANIMALS.

HOW TO DO IT

The receiver gets on their hands and knees. The giver kneels behind them, holding onto the partner's hips for leverage.

WHAT'S GOOD ABOUT IT

Doggie style has a raw, animalistic vibe that makes it one of the most popular sex positions. It offers deep penetration and easier thrusting. Some people like the dominant/subservient aspect of taking someone from behind. And for people who are shy, the lack of eye contact can be a plus.

MAKE IT BETTER

For a tighter feel, have giver put their legs outside of the receiver's and press their legs together.

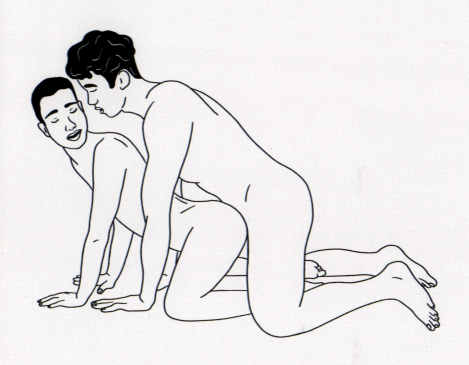

69

IT'S 100 PERCENT PLEASURE.

HOW TO DO IT

One person lies on their back. The other lies on top of their partner, facing their partner's feet. Both people curl their bodies toward each other so that each person's head is near the other person's penis/vulva, semi-resembling a six and a nine.

WHAT'S GOOD ABOUT IT

If simultaneous oral sex is your goal, 69 is pretty much the most direct route to getting body parts where they need to go. It also gives both partners the unique feeling of giving and receiving oral sex at the same time.

MAKE IT BETTER

Make noises to show each other how much you're enjoying them.

Reverse Cowgirl
THE BEST RIDE OF YOUR LIFE.

HOW TO DO IT

The giver lies flat on their back. The receiver straddles the giver's hips, facing their feet and riding their penis or strap-on. The receiver can bend forward and rest on their hands or sit upright.

WHAT'S GOOD ABOUT IT

Works anally or vaginally. If the person on top has a vulva, being on top can be more orgasmic because they can control the speed, motion, and depth and arrange themselves to get more of the clit stimulation they need.

MAKE IT BETTER

The person on top can use hands, a penis stroker, or a vibrator to give themselves more stimulation.

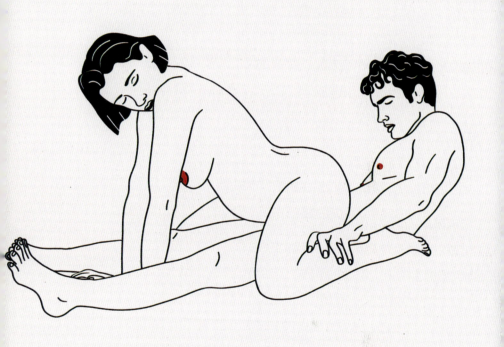

Yab-Yum

OHMMMMMM.

HOW TO DO IT

Sit facing each other. Wrap your arms and legs around each other. For penetrative sex, either hole works—pick a hole and have the receiver sit on their partner's lap.

WHAT'S GOOD ABOUT IT

This is a tantric position for couples to connect on a deeper level. Foster that connected feeling by going slowly, grinding against each other instead of thrusting, and focusing on the gentle movements.

MAKE IT BETTER

Embrace the connection by taking a few moments to place your hands on each other's hearts and sync your breathing. Breathe together and gaze into each other's eyes until you feel connected and/or freaked out by too much eye contact.

Loving Spoons

I AM SO INTO YOU.

HOW TO DO IT

Lie on your sides facing each other. You can intertwine your legs and wrap your arms around each other.

WHAT'S GOOD ABOUT IT

This is an amazing position for sweet romantic sex. There's lots of opportunity for kissing and eye contact, and your hands are free to roam about each other's bodies.

MAKE IT BETTER

Take turns controlling the motion. The giver can thrust, then the receiver can put their leg over their partner's hip and use their leg to rock their partner back and forth to control their movement.

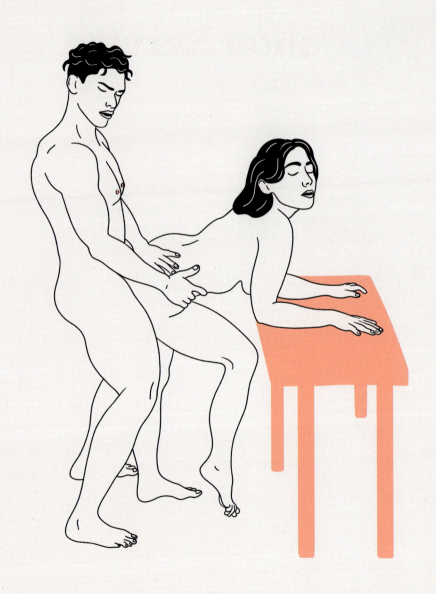

THE BASICS

Counter Service

ONE ORDER OF YOU, PLEASE.

HOW TO DO IT

The receiver stands and bends over a counter or table, resting on their arms with their legs spread. The giver stands behind to enter with a strap-on or penis. Make sure the surface is sturdy and a good height for you.

WHAT'S GOOD ABOUT IT

This position offers penetration with a strong I-must-have-you-now vibe. It's also good for taking sex out of the bedroom. Try it over a kitchen counter, a dining room table, or a bathroom sink.

MAKE IT BETTER

You can add some butt play with a butt plug or the giver's lubed-up finger.

Lazy Dog

DOGGIE STYLE WHEN YOU WANT TO CHILL OUT.

HOW TO DO IT

The receiver lies face down, flat on their stomach with their legs slightly spread. The giver lies on or hunches over their partner and holds themselves up on their elbows. They can penetrate anally or vaginally.

WHAT'S GOOD ABOUT IT

It's got the benefits of doggie style, including deep penetration, but you both get to lie down. Also good for large penises or strap-ons.

MAKE IT BETTER

The receiver can elevate their hips with a pillow so they have room to stroke themselves. If they have a vulva, they can get bonus stimulation by propping a toy on the pillow and pressing against it.

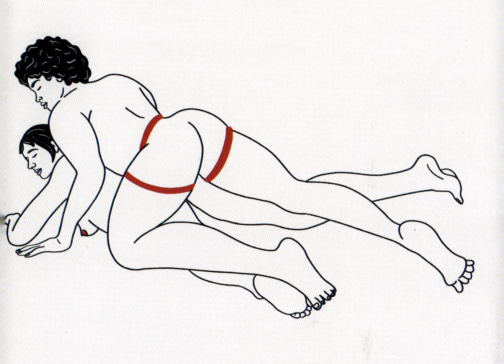

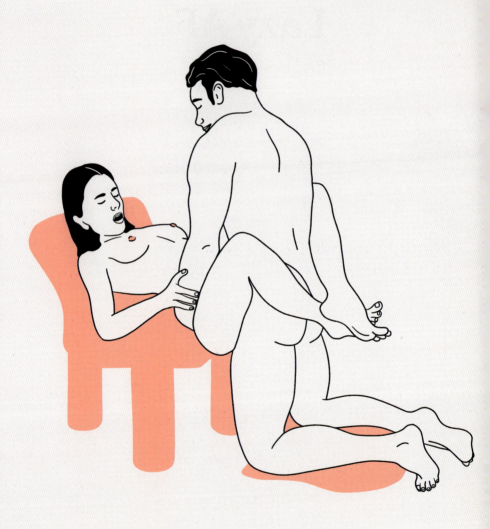

PLEASE BE SEATED

Lazy AF
SEAT-SIDE SERVICE.

HOW TO DO IT

The receiver sits in a comfortable chair and scoots down so their hips are at the edge of the chair. The giver kneels on the floor in front of the chair and the receiver wraps their legs around their partner's hips.

WHAT'S GOOD ABOUT IT

Easy for both partners because one is comfortably sitting and the other is kneeling. Both partners' hands are free to touch themselves or the other person, plus there's lots of eye contact and opportunities for kissing.

MAKE IT BETTER

Instead of looking at each other, watch your bodies connecting with each other. Comment on what you're seeing and tell each other exactly how sexy it looks. Go as loving or dirty as you want.

The Lap Dance
A PRIVATE DANCE.

HOW TO DO IT

The giver sits in a comfortable chair, leans back, and slides their butt toward (or slightly beyond) the edge. The receiver sits in their lap facing away with their legs between their partner's. They can use the chair's arms for leverage.

WHAT'S GOOD ABOUT IT

This is a great position for vaginal or anal sex. Either person can use their hands or a toy to give the receiver clit or penis stimulation.

MAKE IT BETTER

Play up the lap dance part of it. The receiver can start with a strip tease, then tease the giver by grinding against their legs before allowing any penetration.

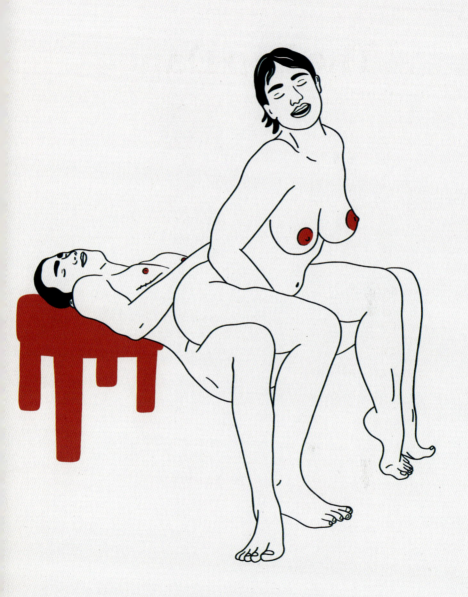

PLEASE BE SEATED

Chair Doggie
HEY, THAT'S NOT HOW YOU'RE SUPPOSED TO USE A CHAIR.

HOW TO DO IT

The receiver kneels in front of a chair and rests their upper body on the chair seat. The giver gets on their knees to enter from behind. The giver puts their legs outside of the receiver's legs. For a tighter feel, the receiver can press their legs tightly together.

WHAT'S GOOD ABOUT IT

It has all the good parts of doggie but is more comfortable for the receiver and provides more stability.

MAKE IT BETTER

If you're on a hard floor, a pillow under each person's knees will make a huge difference.

Best Seat in the House
VIP TREATMENT.

HOW TO DO IT

The receiver sits in a chair, feet flat on the ground in front of them. The giver kneels between their partner's legs and bends down to give them oral sex. The receiver can take control of the action by guiding their partner's head with their hands or just lean back and enjoy.

WHAT'S GOOD ABOUT IT

The giver has their hands free so they can use them to compliment the motions of their mouth. For the receiver, it's *getting to sit down while getting oral.* Doesn't get much better than that.

MAKE IT BETTER

Make it a special treat with a dollop of edible lube.

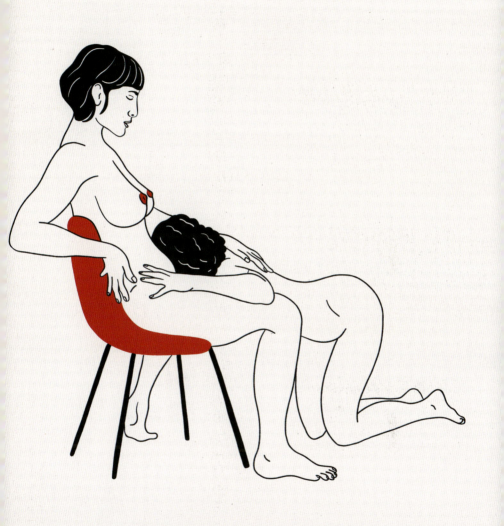

PLEASE BE SEATED

Titanic
FULL SPEED AHEAD.

HOW TO DO IT

The giver sits in a chair, leaning back comfortably. The receiver straddles their partner facing away, then bends their knees and brings their feet back onto the chair. The receiver puts their arms behind them and the giver holds onto their wrist to keep them stable.

WHAT'S GOOD ABOUT IT

Both partners get to work together to pull it off; it's great for anal and vaginal penetration; the giver gets a fine view of their partner's bum; and it's a bit unstable, which gives it an edgy feel.

MAKE IT BETTER

If the receiver is feeling extra flexible, they can lean forward toward the ground to gift the giver a porn-worthy view.

Stand and Deliver
THIS IS SO HAPPENING.

HOW TO DO IT

Both partners stand facing each other. The receiver wraps their arms around their partner's neck and one leg around their hips.

WHAT'S GOOD ABOUT IT

The position works well as a quickie when you absolutely have to get your hands on each other this...very...second.

MAKE IT BETTER

This is a hard position to maintain for a long time, so make it easier on yourselves by having one of you lean back against a wall or counter. And if a penis or strap-on is involved, try a vibrating cock ring to amp up the stimulation.

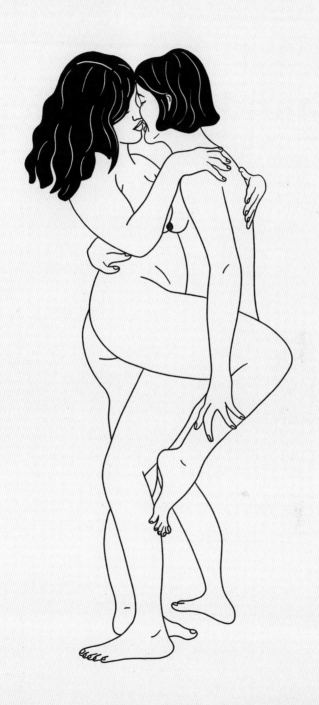

Standing Room Only

KNOCK, KNOCK.

HOW TO DO IT

The giver leans back with their upper back against a doorjamb and their legs stretching to the other side of the door. The receiver stands, straddles their partner, and wraps their arms around their neck.

WHAT'S GOOD ABOUT IT

Standing positions can be hard, but this one is easier to maintain because the giver has a sturdy surface to lean against. It's also a good standing position for people with big height differences because you can adjust to get things where they need to go.

MAKE IT BETTER

Try an arousal gel or a heated or cooling lube to intensify the experience.

I Must Have You Now

LIKE A SEXY JUNGLE GYM.

HOW TO DO IT

The giver leans back against a wall with their feet firmly on the ground. While the giver is holding them by their butt, the receiver puts their arms around their partner's neck and walks up the wall until their feet are next to their partner's hips. The giver holds onto their partner, keeping them aloft while the receiver clings to the giver, clenching their legs around them.

WHAT'S GOOD ABOUT IT

The carrying aspect is very swoon-worthy and romance novel-like, plus the giver can thrust deeply.

MAKE IT BETTER

Instead of having the giver thrust, the receiver can use their feet to direct the movement and, if the giver has a vulva, they can squeeze their pelvic muscles with each thrust.

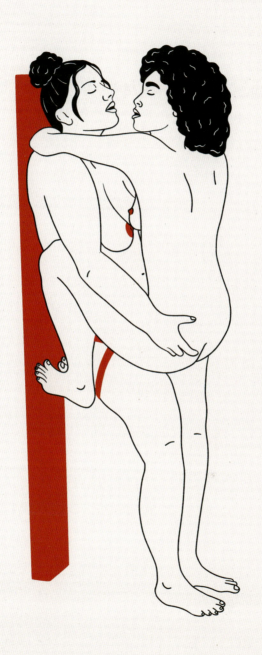

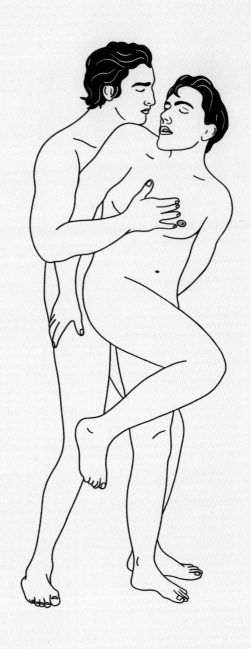

The Pat-Down

HOLD IT RIGHT THERE. GONNA NEED TO CHECK YOU OUT.

HOW TO DO IT

The giver stands and the receiver backs up against their partner, lifting one leg up. The receiver holds onto the partner's leg or chest.

WHAT'S GOOD ABOUT IT

This is an excellent anal position since, hey, the butt is already right there. And the receiver's hands are free to stroke themselves.

MAKE IT BETTER

If you both are down for it, try some role-play as a police officer and suspect. Need a plotline? The officer frisks the suspect for contraband but takes it *much* farther than the police handbook recommends.

Leg Day

HOPE Y'ALL HAVE BEEN DOING THOSE WALL SQUATS.

HOW TO DO IT

The giver leans their back against a doorjamb and slides their body down so that they have their back against the doorjamb and their knees bent. The receiver straddles their partner and perches on the giver's upper thighs. The receiver keeps their feet on the ground for leverage.

WHAT'S GOOD ABOUT IT

This pose feels intense and animalistic. The receiver gets to control the speed, depth, and angles of the thrusts.

MAKE IT BETTER

If you do really like doing it in doorway but don't have the quads for it, invest in a sex swing that hangs from the doorjamb for gravity-defying orgasms.

STANDING O

Back That Azz UP
WE'RE GOING DEEP.

HOW TO DO IT

The giver leans back against a doorjamb, bracing themselves by holding onto the doorframe overhead. Their feet are a foot or two (30 to 60 cm) in front of them. The receiver straddles their partner, facing away and holding onto the other side of the doorframe.

WHAT'S GOOD ABOUT IT

This position allows both people to have something to hold onto and gives them some leverage while they both enjoy deep, heavy-duty penetration.

MAKE IT BETTER

Applying a CBD-based lube or oil about 15 minutes before penetration can enhance the sensations in the receiver's vagina or butt.

The Tree House

WHEN YOU'RE CLIMBING THE WALLS FOR EACH OTHER.

HOW TO DO IT

Stand facing each other next to a sturdy counter, chair, or couch, each of you holding on with one hand. The giver bends their leg up so that the receiver can hold it up. The receiver lifts their leg on the same side up and over the giver's lifted leg.

WHAT'S GOOD ABOUT IT

The mutual leg lift adds a little twist for a new angle of penetration.

MAKE IT BETTER

For a nonpenetrative option, the receiver can hump the giver's leg, or you can slide a vibrating toy between you and let it work on both of you.

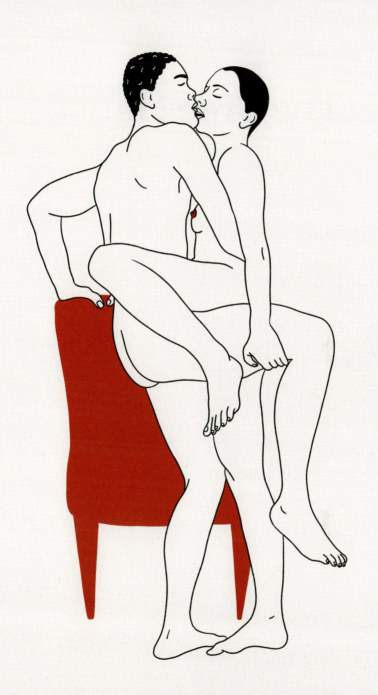

TWEAKS THAT CHANGE EVERYTHING

Gender Is a Construct Missionary

FLIP MISSIONARY OVER.

HOW TO DO IT

The giver lies on their back with their legs spread. The receiver lies on top between their partner's legs. The receiver holds themselves up on their forearms and holds their partner's hands.

WHAT'S GOOD ABOUT IT

This is a great way to break out of roles such as top/bottom, dominant/submissive, and man penetrator/woman penetrated. Changing that dynamic lets the receiver be the dominant player and kicks you out of any ruts you might be stuck in.

MAKE IT BETTER

Go further with the dom/sub vibe and have the person on top pin their partner's arms down, talk dirty to them, or just selfishly take their own pleasure.

Pressed Missionary
IF MISSIONARY NEVER *QUITE* DOES IT FOR YOU.

HOW TO DO IT

The giver is on the top and the receiver is on the bottom, à la regular missionary, but the receiver puts their legs inside the giver's legs and presses their legs tightly together.

WHAT'S GOOD ABOUT IT

This position has a tighter feel than missionary, and if the receiver has a vulva, this allows them to angle themselves so that each stroke of their partner's penis or strap-on rubs over their clit.

MAKE IT BETTER

Instead of the giver thrusting, the receiver can roll their hips and grind against their partner's penis or strap-on.

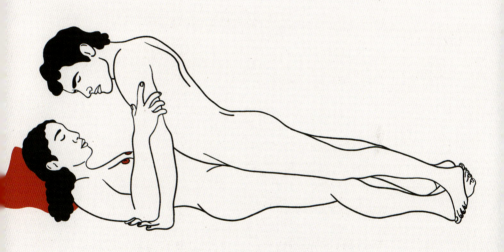

Flying V

V AS IN VOYEURISTIC.

HOW TO DO IT

The receiver lies flat on their back with their legs straight up in a V shape. The giver kneels to enter, holding onto the receiver's ankles.

WHAT'S GOOD ABOUT IT

The giver gets a stellar view of their partner and the sight of their penis or strap-on moving inside them. Plus, the receiver has their hands free to touch themselves.

MAKE IT BETTER

The giver can move the receiver's legs to change the angle and sensations. Try pressing the receiver's legs tightly together, open and shut like scissors, off to one side, or rocking their hips up and down to hit more internal spots.

CAT Power

SCIENTIFICALLY PROVEN TO BE MORE ORGASMIC FOR PEOPLE WITH VULVAS. #FACTS

HOW TO DO IT

The receiver lies on their back. The giver mounts them, moving upward on their partner's body so that their penis or strap-on points downward and the top rubs against their partner's clitoris. The giver grinds their pubic bone against their partner's clitoris.

WHAT'S GOOD ABOUT IT

Coital Alignment Technique (CAT) can help receivers with vulvas be more orgasmic (or orgasmic in the first place) with penetrative sex because there's more direct contact with the clit.

MAKE IT BETTER

Grind slowly and use a ton of lube, taking time to make sure the receiver is well aroused and getting the stimulation they need. If penetration isn't orgasmic for them (totally normal!), partner the CAT with oral or a lubed hand.

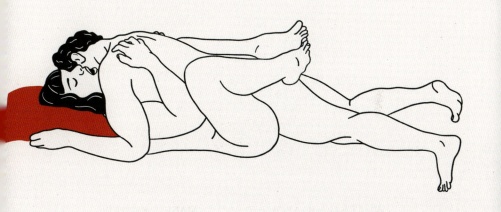

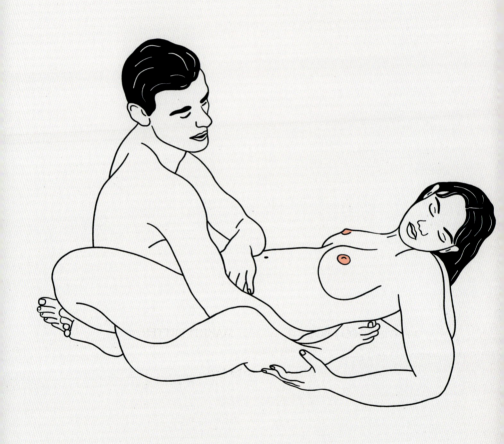

TWEAKS THAT CHANGE EVERYTHING

Slow Jam
RAISE THE ROOF.

HOW TO DO IT

The giver sits with their legs crossed, and the receiver sits on their partner's lap straddling them, legs wrapped behind their hips. Then the receiver leans full back onto their elbows, keeping their legs wrapped around their partner's hips.

WHAT'S GOOD ABOUT IT

This position is great for giving internal stimulation to the giver's G-spot (a sensitive part of the upper wall of the vagina) or the P-spot (the upper wall of the anus where the prostate gland is).

MAKE IT BETTER

The giver can (nay, should!) reach for their partner's penis or vulva to rub it while they're inside to give their partner intense dual stimulation.

The Love Seat

GO THIGH HIGH.

HOW TO DO IT

The giver lies back on a bed or cushy carpet and lifts their legs up, bending their knees to their chest. The receiver faces away and slowly (and carefully!) sits on the backs of their partner's thighs with their feet in front of them.

WHAT'S GOOD ABOUT IT

Whether used as an anal or vaginal position, this gives the receiver lots of room to rub themselves or use a favorite toy.

MAKE IT BETTER

For more intense thrusting as you get closer to orgasm, the receiver can get more leverage by moving their legs so that they're on their knees.

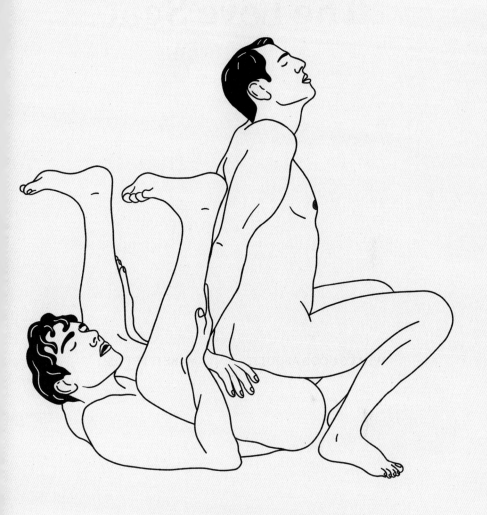

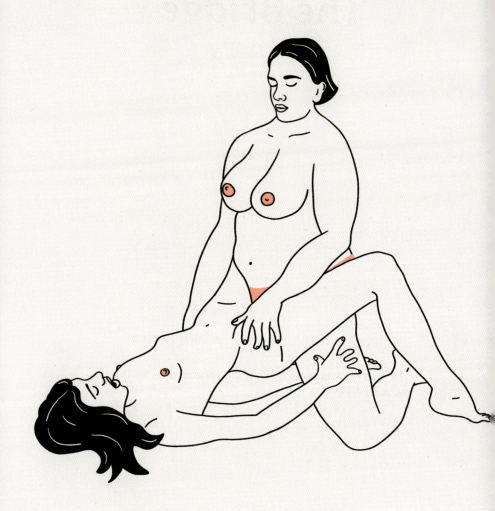

The Bridge
PRESS 'N PLAY.

HOW TO DO IT

The receiver lies on their back, plants their feet about hip distance apart, and lifts their hips so that they're in the bridge yoga position. The giver kneels between their partner's legs to enter.

WHAT'S GOOD ABOUT IT

The giver has lots of room for deep thrusting and/or side-to-side grinding and the receiver can press their pelvis upward if/when they want their partner to go deeper.

MAKE IT BETTER

If the penetration is too deep or intense for the receiver, they can make an "okay" symbol with their forefinger and thumb to encircle the penis or strap-on. Add more fingers for more of a buffer.

The Windshield Wipers

SWIPE RIGHT (THEN LEFT, THEN RIGHT).

HOW TO DO IT

The receiver lies on their back with their legs raised straight up. The giver kneels by their partner's butt with their knees spread wide. The giver holds onto their partner's legs by the ankles, pressing them both on one side of their body to the other.

WHAT'S GOOD ABOUT IT

Shifting the legs changes the angle of stimulation and if the receiver has a vagina, the motion will make the vagina naturally squeeze around the penis or strap-on.

MAKE IT BETTER

The giver can kiss their partner's feet and ankles and suck on their toes.

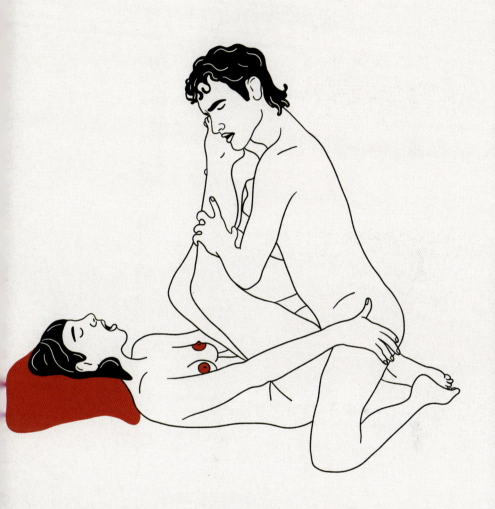

TWEAKS THAT CHANGE EVERYTHING

The Snake Charmer

ENCHANT EACH OTHER.

HOW TO DO IT

The giver sits at the edge of a bed with feet on the floor. The receiver straddles them facing away and leaning forward, with hands on their partner's knees and legs bent back on the bed. The receiver raises themselves with their hands à la the cobra yoga position.

WHAT'S GOOD ABOUT IT

This is a sexy way to get a new angle of penetration. The giver can squeeze their partner's butt and reach around to rub and pinch their nipples.

MAKE IT BETTER

For even deeper penetration, the receiver can lean all the way forward and put their hands on the floor.

Sideways 69

LUXURIATE IN EACH OTHER.

HOW TO DO IT

Lie on your side facing your partner, with your mouth to the other person's groin. Spread your knees and put your top leg over your partner's head to give them better access.

WHAT'S GOOD ABOUT IT

Give and get oral sex at the same time while getting to lie down comfortably. Win-win!

MAKE IT BETTER

If giving and getting at the same time is too much multitasking, take turns being the one giving more intense sex oral. The person receiving can really focus on the sensations without having to think about simultaneously giving stellar oral.

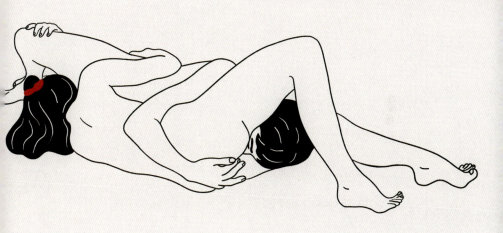

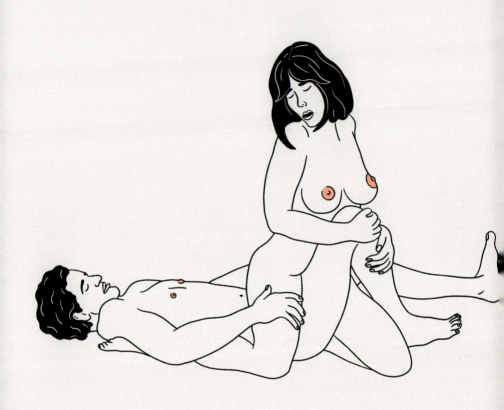

The Humper

FOR THOSE WHO HAVE KNOWN THE LOVE OF A GOOD PILLOW.

HOW TO DO IT

The giver lies on their back with one knee bent up. The receiver straddles their partner's bent leg, facing away from them, then lowers themselves for penetration. The receiver presses their vulva or the underside of their penis and rubs against their partner's thrust as they thrust and grind.

WHAT'S GOOD ABOUT IT

This is great for people who learned to orgasm while humping a pillow, stuffed animal, or their hand because it mimics the motion.

MAKE IT BETTER

For a sexy, slippery feel, cover the giver's leg in lube so the receiver can glide smoothly over their partner's thigh.

Sealed with a Twist
A KIND OF SPOONING-DOGGIE HYBRID.

HOW TO DO IT

The receiver lies on their side, head comfortably on a pillow. The giver is behind, holding themselves up on their hands, with one behind their partner and one in front. The giver slides a leg in between their partner's leg and enters from behind.

WHAT'S GOOD ABOUT IT

Whether anally or vaginally, this position combines the deep penetration of doggie with the comfort and closeness of spooning.

MAKE IT BETTER

If the receiver has a vulva, the giver can press their thigh firmly against their partner for extra clit stimulation.

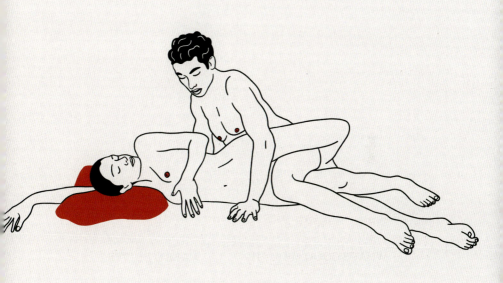

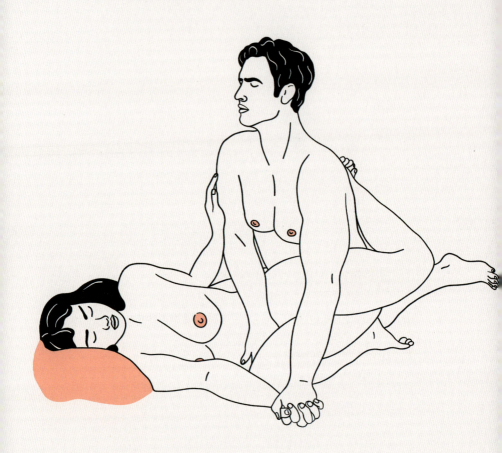

THE INTERMEDIATE LEVEL

Twister

LEFT FOOT RED, RIGHT HAND GROIN.

HOW TO DO IT

The receiver lies on their side. The giver kneels to enter, straddling their partner's lower leg. The receiver lifts their upper leg and curls it around their partner's back.

WHAT'S GOOD ABOUT IT

This gives a new sideways angle of penetration, plus the option of eye contact or no eye contact, depending on how y'all feel.

MAKE IT BETTER

The giver can make it feel much more intimate by holding hands, using the other hand to stroke their vulva or penis, and whispering sweet, sexy words.

THE SEX POSITION PLAYBOOK

Splitting of Bamboo
BLAST FROM THE PAST.

HOW TO DO IT

The receiver lies on their back with one leg on their partner's shoulders. The giver kneels, sitting down on their feet by their partner's bum to enter. The receiver switches between which leg they lift.

WHAT'S GOOD ABOUT IT

This is an ancient Kama Sutra position that was geared for male-female sex. The text recommends the receiver tighten their yoni (vagina) around their partner's lingam (penis) every time they switch from one leg to another. But the receiver can tighten a yoni or an anus.

MAKE IT BETTER

Have the giver give the receiver a hand job and switch up the motion with each leg switch.

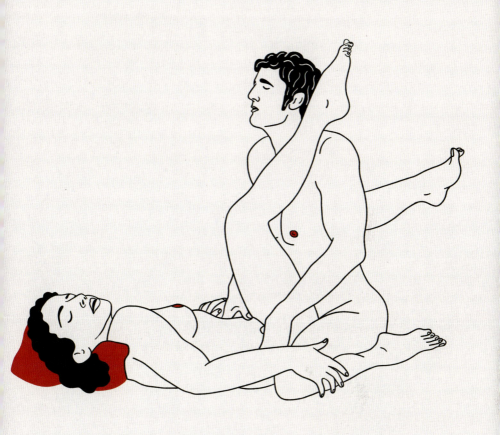

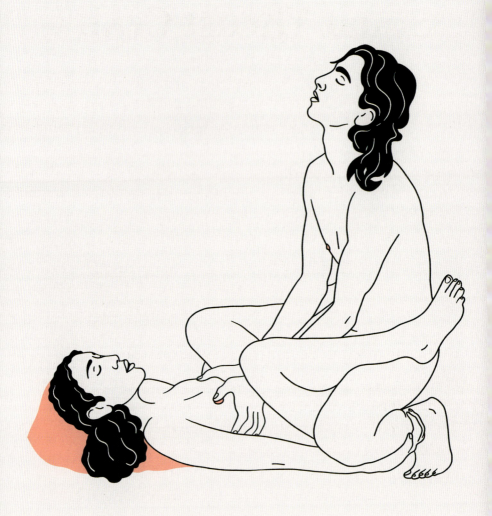

THE INTERMEDIATE LEVEL

Squat Thrust Crab

SEX ON THE HALF SHELL.

HOW TO DO IT

The receiver lies on their back, head comfortably on a pillow, with their legs spread and knees bent. The giver squats between their partner's legs and their receiver puts their legs over their partner's thighs.

WHAT'S GOOD ABOUT IT

This position has a primal, rutting vibe and gives both partners a good view of what's going on.

MAKE IT BETTER

The receiver has their hands free to rub themselves or, if their partner has a penis, they can put two fingers on either side of their partner's penis to give them bonus stimulation with each thrust.

The Mmmm
BUMP AND GRIND.

HOW TO DO IT

The giver kneels, then leans back on their hands and rests their butt on their feet. The receiver faces away and straddles their partner, holding themselves on their hands and knees.

WHAT'S GOOD ABOUT IT

This position gives the receiver great leverage for fast and intense thrusting. And if the giver is into butts, they've got easy access.

MAKE IT BETTER

Make it more intimate by slowing it way down. The receiver can rock their hips slowly, drawing out the experience and letting both of you enjoy every bump and grind.

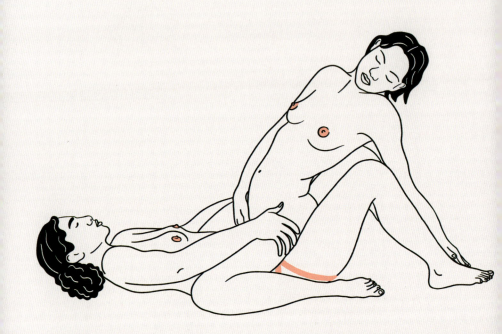

THE INTERMEDIATE LEVEL

Saddleback
SHOW THEM HOW IT'S DONE.

HOW TO DO IT

The giver lies on their back with their knees bent. The receiver straddles their partner, then places one hand back and leans backward to rest on the giver's thighs.

WHAT'S GOOD ABOUT IT

The receiver has a hand free so they can rub themselves as they move.

MAKE IT BETTER

This a great opportunity for the receiver to put on a bit of a show for the giver. They can lean back and let their partner watch as they stroke themselves to and through an orgasm. The giver can thrust upward or just lie back and watch their partner in the throes.

The Hot Seat

SO. VERY. INTIMATE.

HOW TO DO IT

The giver kneels and sits back on their feet. The receiver straddles their partner and sits on the giver's legs, feet on the ground. Both partners wrap their arms around each other to keep the receiver steady as the receiver slides up and down.

WHAT'S GOOD ABOUT IT

This is an intimate position with lots of skin-to-skin contact, plus opportunities for gazing lustfully at each other and long, slow kisses.

MAKE IT BETTER

Try this in ultra slow motion. Draw it out as long as possible by moving very slowly and taking time to kiss, suck on each other's earlobes, and lick each other's nipples.

THE INTERMEDIATE LEVEL

Indecent Proposal
I DO.

HOW TO DO IT

The receiver kneels on a soft surface with their knees about hip distance apart. The giver kneels in front of them on one bended knee, as though they are proposing.

WHAT'S GOOD ABOUT IT

This "marriage" is like a union of equals. The partners are facing each other and can both thrust together or stay still and let the other person control how fast the movement is.

MAKE IT BETTER

If you have a big height difference, a sex wedge or a stack of firm pillows under the shorter one can help you get body parts where they need to go.

The Rocking Horse
RIDE A COCKHORSE TO BANBURY CROSS.

HOW TO DO IT

The giver kneels, then leans back on their hands and sits back on their feet. The receiver straddles their partner, squatting with their weight on the balls of their feet and holding onto their partner's hips.

WHAT'S GOOD ABOUT IT

This position gives the receiver lots of room for controlling the speed, depth, and rhythm of the movement. This is especially good for anal when the receiver needs to take their time to ease a penis or strap-on inside them.

MAKE IT BETTER

If the receiver has a vulva, they can get more clit stimulation by rocking and grinding back and forth while pressing against their partner's pubic bone.

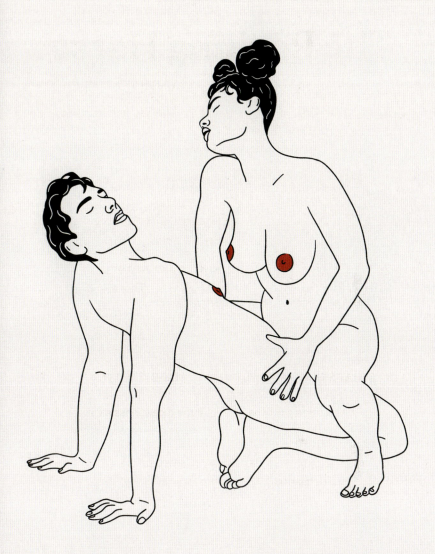

THE INTERMEDIATE LEVEL

Supercharged 69
FIRE UP THE TOYS AND GOOOOOOO.

HOW TO DO IT

Lie on your sides facing each other in a sideways 69 position, with one person's head toward the other one's feet. Instead of oral sex, use toys on each other.

WHAT'S GOOD ABOUT IT

Outsourcing the 69ing to the toys allows you to focus on the good vibes between your legs while getting an up-close view of your partner getting simultaneously ravished via toy.

MAKE IT BETTER

Decide beforehand that you're going to pick out toys for one another. You can keep your choices a surprise or build anticipation by letting each other know a few days or hours in advance what awaits them.

Slip 'n Slide

SLIPPERY WHEN WET.

HOW TO DO IT

Throw down some old towels or sheets, then cover yourselves in an excessive amount of massage oil. Take turns lying on the other person's back and slipping and sliding against their body.

WHAT'S GOOD ABOUT IT

This is a warm-up move that's part silly and fun and part sexy body contact. You can turn over and rub your chests against each other or re-create the desperate lust of early make-out sessions by grinding against each other.

MAKE IT BETTER

You can use this as a prelude to penetration or, for a nonpenetrative option, move onto slippery masturbation—touching each other or yourself.

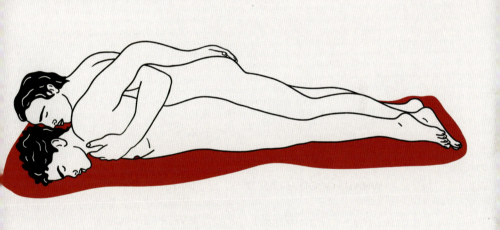

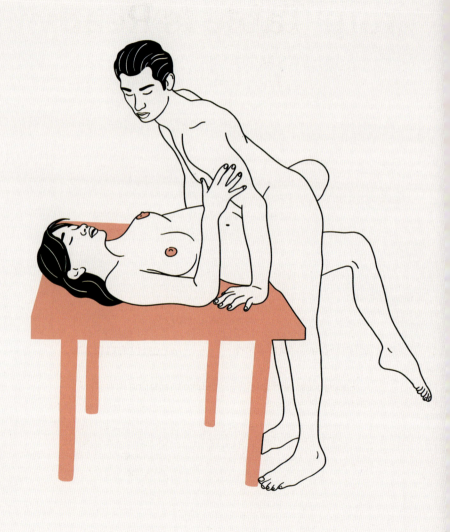

THE INTERMEDIATE LEVEL

Your Table Is Ready

YOU: IT'S WHAT'S FOR DINNER.

HOW TO DO IT

The receiver lies on their back on a table with their hips at the edge and a leg on a chair for leverage, if wanted. The giver stands to enter, resting their hands on the table, either straddling their partner's leg or standing between them.

WHAT'S GOOD ABOUT IT

Easy access and solid G-spot or P-spot stim, and the receiver has their hands free to touch themselves.

MAKE IT BETTER

Take the eating theme more literally by having the giver pull up a chair to give the receiver a full course of oral sex. Go all-in with lickable add-ons like chocolate syrup and whipped cream. (Just keep 'em out of vaginas.)

Froggie Style
HOP TO IT.

HOW TO DO IT

The giver lies on their back with their legs slightly spread and knees bent. The receiver squats over them, facing away, and lowers themselves onto their partner's penis or strap-on. The receiver puts their hands in front of them on the bed for balance.

 WHAT'S GOOD ABOUT IT

The receiver gets lots of control of the movement and depth of the penetration, which is especially helpful for the receiver if it's anal sex or they have some pain with vaginal sex.

 MAKE IT BETTER

Add some butt play by having the giver slide a lubed-up finger around and in the receiver's butthole.

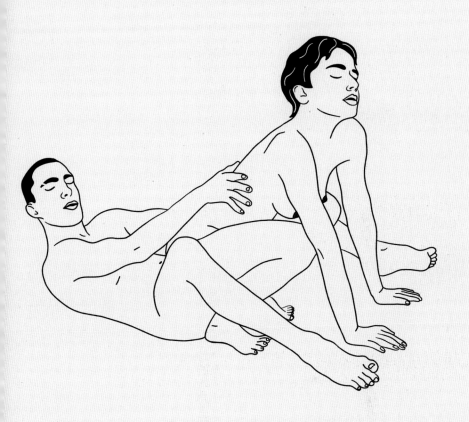

THE INTERMEDIATE LEVEL

T-Top

RIDE LIKE THE WIND.

HOW TO DO IT

The receiver lies on their back with their legs straight up in the air. The giver lies perpendicularly to enter so that the two are forming a *T* shape, and the giver raises one arm to simulate a feeling of flying. The receiver slides an anal plug into their partner.

WHAT'S GOOD ABOUT IT

The one-handedness of the position provides the giver a feeling of weightlessness, but the anal plug grounds them so they get to experience both sensations at once.

MAKE IT BETTER

No reason the giver gets to be the only one plugged up. The receiver can pop in a vibrating anal plug and let it rumble away.

THE SEX POSITION PLAYBOOK

Titty F*ck
GET ME AT 'EM.

HOW TO DO IT

The receiver lies on their back and the giver straddles them, penis or strap-on at the receiver's chest level. The receiver lubes up their hands and chest and squeezes their boobs around their partner's member, then curls their hand over the top to form a tight tube.

WHAT'S GOOD ABOUT IT

This doesn't require big boobs and can be done by any gender—just use more hand to form the tube.

MAKE IT BETTER

If the person on top has a vulva, they can grind against their partner's chest while their partner slides two lubed fingers on either side of their clit.

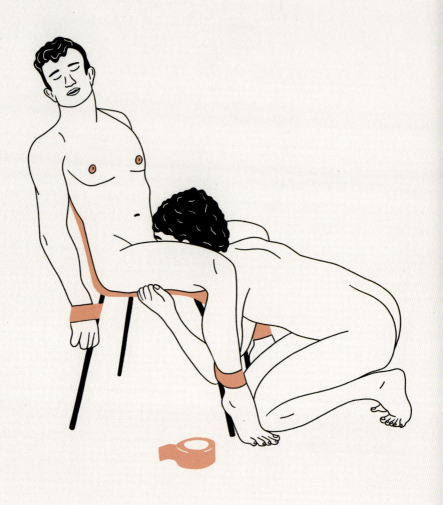

All Tied Up

MY WILL BE DONE.

HOW TO DO IT

The receiver sits in a chair, ankles tied to the chair legs and wrists bound behind them. The giver kneels between their legs to give them oral.

WHAT'S GOOD ABOUT IT

The dom and sub dynamic intensifies the experience for both. And for the receiver, being tied up is a great way to get out of their head and relax into the experience.

MAKE IT BETTER

The dom can lean into their role by issuing commands like "Open your legs for me," "Let me hear you moan," or "Beg me to touch you."

You Shall Service Me
AS I LIKE IT.

HOW TO DO IT

The receiver stands with their legs slightly spread. The giver kneels before them with their hands bound behind them and gives oral to the receiver as they are commanded to.

WHAT'S GOOD ABOUT IT

The dom/sub aspect allows the receiver to get exactly the stimulation they need by directing their partner and lets the giver submit entirely to pleasing their partner. And kneeling before someone furthers the subservient vibe.

MAKE IT BETTER

The receiver can take complete control by holding onto the giver's head and directing the motion, adding instructions as they guide.

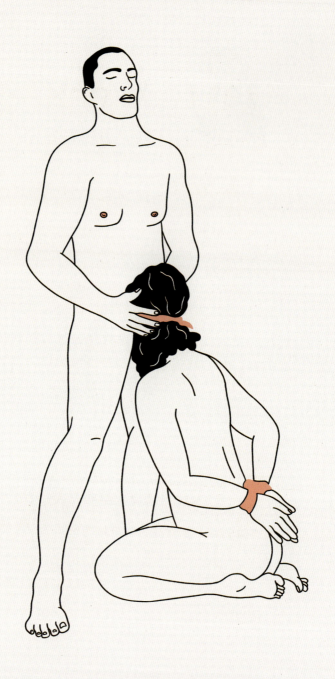

Get to Work

A FACE F*CK, TBH.

HOW TO DO IT

The giver kneels with their wrists tied behind them and blindfolded. The receiver stands before their partner and presses their penis or vulva into or against their partner's mouth. The giver keeps their head still so the receiver can move against their mouth.

WHAT'S GOOD ABOUT IT

The blindfolded giver gets the heady (er...) experience of their partner's penis or vulva using only taste, sound, scent, and touch. The receiver gets a *very* personal assistant to do their bidding.

MAKE IT BETTER

If you want to go hard with the BDSM aspects, the receiver can gently swat the giver's back with a flogger and/or say degrading things. (Enthusiastic consent, as always, is a must.)

Bend Over and Take It

YOU GET WHAT YOU GET.

HOW TO DO IT

The receiver puts their head and hands down on the floor, using a pillow for comfort and making sure their head and neck are fully supported, and puts their feet on the floor behind them. The giver stands to enter from behind, holding on to the receiver's hips to hold them steady.

WHAT'S GOOD ABOUT IT

The receiver has little control with what's happening, which works well within a dom/sub scenario.

MAKE IT BETTER

After the giver takes their own pleasure (that's part of the whole deal with this), if the receiver needs more than penetration to have an orgasm, the giver can return the favor with an attentive hand job.

In Your Face

HELLO, GORGEOUS.

HOW TO DO IT

The giver lies comfortably on their back, knees bent, head on a pillow if they'd like. The receiver gets on their hands and knees and bends down so that their penis or vulva is next to their partner's mouth. The receiver rides their partner's mouth and face. (The receiver is doing more of a hover than a full face sit so that the giver can do helpful things like continue to breathe.)

WHAT'S GOOD ABOUT IT

The receiver uses their partner's mouth however they want. If y'all are shy, this one has the advantage of no eye contact.

MAKE IT BETTER

The giver can use their hands to play with their partner's butt, balls, or outer lips.

The Spanking Machine
YOU HAVE BEEN VERY, VERY BAD.

HOW TO DO IT

The giver sits at the edge of a bed or with feet on the floor. The receiver faces away, wraps their legs around their partner's waist, and leans forward until their hands are on the floor. The giver alternates between thrusts and spanks.

WHAT'S GOOD ABOUT IT

Pain can heighten arousal, and the mixture of pain and pleasure can make it even more intense. As long as one of you is happy being the spanker and the other the spankee, go to town.

MAKE IT BETTER

Try edging, where the giver brings the receiver *just* to the edge of orgasm, then stops. Repeat till the receiver is speaking in tongues.

Sex Doll

YOUR WISH IS MY COMMAND.

HOW TO DO IT

The giver sits in a chair leaning back with their hips at the edge. The receiver lies over their partner's legs with their hands on the floor and their legs spread and behind their partner.

WHAT'S GOOD ABOUT IT

This works for dom/sub play because the receiver is in an inherently subservient position—even more so if the giver holds onto the receiver's hips to use their body (again, consensually) like a sex doll or Fleshlight.

MAKE IT BETTER

Instead of having the giver move the receiver's hips, they can command the receiver to do their bidding (e.g., "Shake that ass for me" or "Faster. Now.").

Face/Off

ROW, ROW, ROW YOUR BOAT.

HOW TO DO IT

The giver sits with their legs outstretched in front of them. The receiver sits on their partner's lap, facing them, with their legs outstretched around their partner. The giver holds onto the receiver's waist, and the receiver holds onto the giver's shoulders. Use each other as leverage to sway back and forth.

WHAT'S GOOD ABOUT IT

If jackhammer thrusting is not your jam, this is a good alternative, with gentle rocking motions and grinding against each other.

MAKE IT BETTER

If both partners have a vulva, this position pairs well with a flexible, double-headed vibrator.

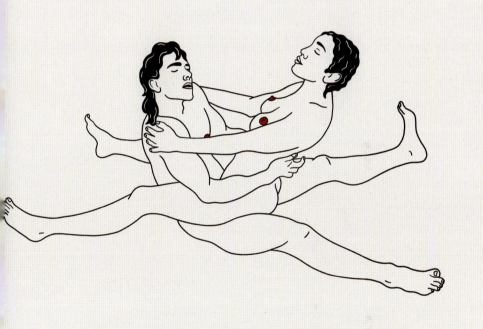

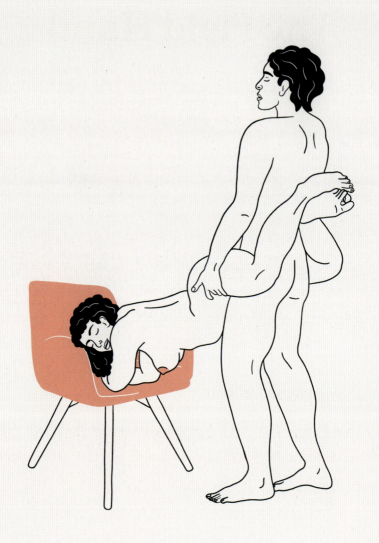

ADVANCED MODE

The Field Hand

LIKE WHEELBARROW RACES AT THE COMPANY PICNIC, BUT NAKED AND WITH SEX.

HOW TO DO IT

The receiver starts by kneeling in front of a (sturdy!) chair or bed with their weight resting on their elbows and forearms. The giver stands behind their partner and lifts them by their hips, raising them to waist level. The receiver wraps their legs behind their partner's back to help bear some of their weight.

WHAT'S GOOD ABOUT IT

This one offers about the deepest penetration allowed by law.

MAKE IT BETTER

If the receiver has a vulva, they can pull their partner in deeper with their legs and pause for a moment to pulse their Kegel muscles for a tighter feel.

The Sculpture
AREN'T Y'ALL FANCY?

HOW TO DO IT

The giver gets on one knee next to a bed, with the other leg bent in front of them. They have one hand on the bed, the other holding their partner's thigh. The receiver kneels on the opposite leg, lifts the other leg over their partner's bent knee, and leans forward so that their arm is resting on the bed.

WHAT'S GOOD ABOUT IT

The bed gives both of you something to hang onto for deep thrusts and extremely deep penetration, either anally or vaginally.

MAKE IT BETTER

Put a couple pillows under both of your knees for maximum comfort.

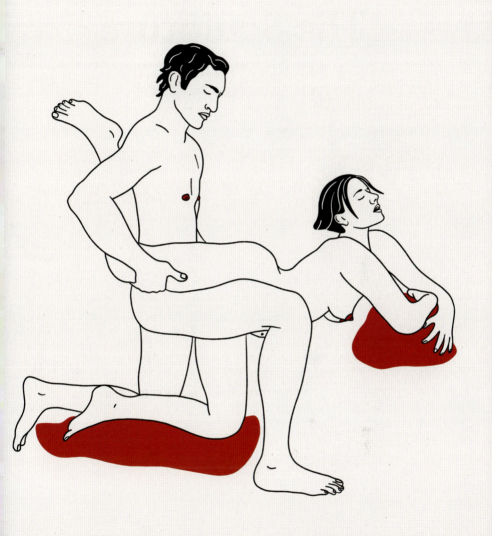

ADVANCED MODE

X Marks the Spot
THAT BURIED TREASURE? YOU.

HOW TO DO IT

The giver lays straight, holding themselves up on their hands. The receiver lies in the opposite direction, facing their partner's feet, straddling their partner, and holding themselves up with straight arms. Their bodies cross in the middle.

WHAT'S GOOD ABOUT IT

This is a rare sex position that offers truly equal opportunity to control the speed and depth of the thrusting. One person can take charge while the other is still, both can move at once, or you can take turns.

MAKE IT BETTER

If someone's arms aren't up to the task (that would be most of us), it's easy to modify midposition. The giver can lower their butt and/or the receiver can rest their weight on their knees.

The Lawn Mower
RIDE THAT SEXY MOWER.

HOW TO DO IT

The receiver rests their forearms on a pillow. The giver lifts the receiver's body up by the hips to enter and the receiver wraps their legs back around their partner's waist.

WHAT'S GOOD ABOUT IT

This is a challenging position that allows the giver to arrange their partner's body exactly how they want it. Plus, you get bragging rights that you did it.

MAKE IT BETTER

Give that receiver a reward for their fine feat of athleticism with a generous dose of oral sex. Lower them to their knees so the giver can kneel to lick and kiss from behind.

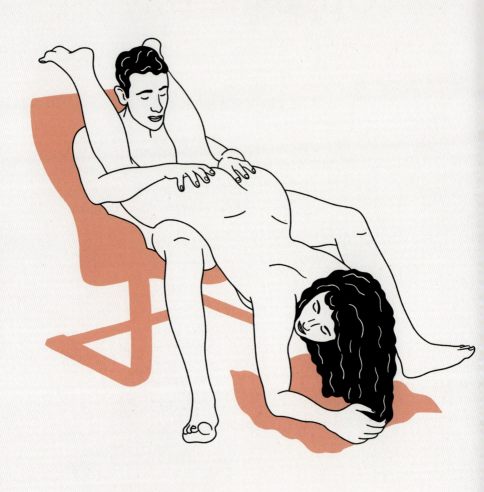

ADVANCED MODE

Opposite Day
IMPROPER CHAIR USAGE.

HOW TO DO IT

The giver sits in a chair. The receiver lies down over their partner's body with their elbows and forearms on a pillow on the floor in front of the chair and their legs back so that their knees are on the partner's chest and their feet back on either side of their partner's head.

WHAT'S GOOD ABOUT IT

The giver gets an incredible view and feel of their partner's body draped over them. The receiver gets directed internal stimulation to the lower wall of the vagina or anus.

MAKE IT BETTER

This lends well to all kinds of butt play including squeezing and massaging the ass cheeks, butt plugs, anal beads, or using fingers.

The Launch Pad

HOLD THE HELL ON.

HOW TO DO IT

Start in a sitting position with the receiver sitting on the giver's lap, facing away from them. The giver then stands slowly, holding onto the receiver's arms. The receiver bends their knees and wraps their feet around the back of the giver's thighs while the giver stands, holding onto the receiver's forearms. Try it over a bed in case it doesn't work out *quite* like the picture.

WHAT'S GOOD ABOUT IT

Doing hard things brings you closer as a couple. And this, my friend, is one of those hard things.

MAKE IT BETTER

This one *really* depends on a tight grip, so lube up beforehand, then wash your hands before any hoisting happens.

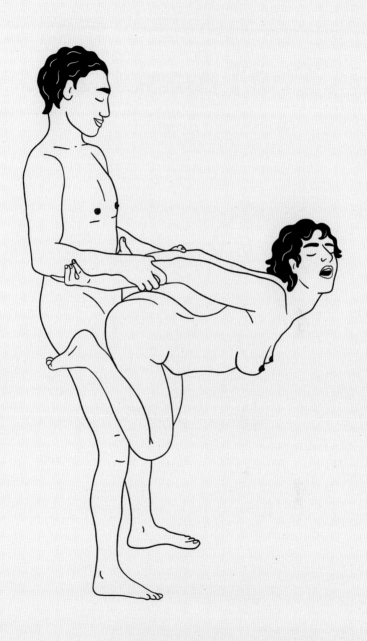

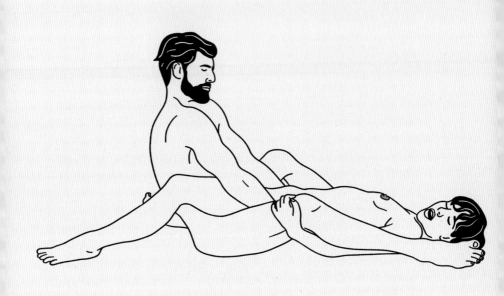

ADVANCED MODE

The Pretzel

TIE YOURSELVES IN KNOTS.

HOW TO DO IT

The giver sits with their legs straight in front of them. The receiver lies on their back with their legs spread and feet behind their partner's butt.

WHAT'S GOOD ABOUT IT

The giver can thrust upward or hold onto their partner's hands to rock them back and forth. The receiver can rub themselves while being penetrated for double stimulation.

MAKE IT BETTER

Try making it a more connected experience by watching each other's faces as you move. Don't even talk—just let each other know how much you're into it via moans and sighs.

Have a Seat
BUTTY LOVE.

HOW TO DO IT

The receiver gets on their knees then lowers the top of their body and turns their body so they're resting on one shoulder and their head. Facing away from the receiver, the giver squats down so that they're penetrating the receiver anally.

WHAT'S GOOD ABOUT IT

Both people get the pleasure of anal sex from their side of the equation, plus the giver gets to indulge any voyeuristic tendencies by watching themselves slide in and out of their partner.

MAKE IT BETTER

The receiver has a free hand to amp up their own stimulation by stroking themselves or using their favorite toy.

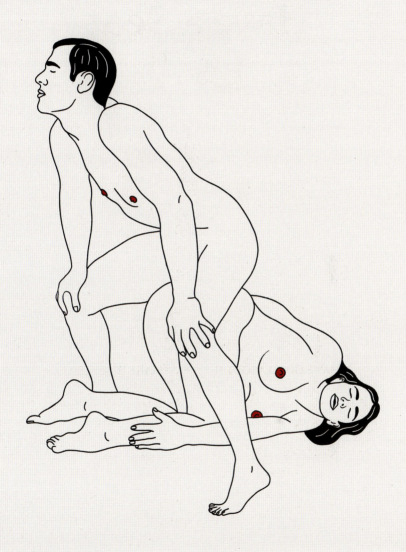

ADVANCED MODE

The Beach Chair
THE SEAT OF PLEASURE.

HOW TO DO IT

The giver squats so that they're resting on the balls of their feet and their thighs are forming a seat for their partner. The receiver sits on their partner's thighs, facing the giver. Wrap your arms around each other.

WHAT'S GOOD ABOUT IT

You can switch back and forth between who is in control. The giver can rock back and forth on their heels, holding their partner, or the giver can take control of the rocking or move up and down using their feet for leverage.

MAKE IT BETTER

Embrace the embracing of it. Hug tightly together, pressing your chests against each other and kiss each other's necks, lips, and ears.

The Hokey Pokey
YOU PUT YOUR WHOLE SELF IN.

HOW TO DO IT

Lie on your sides facing each other, with each person's head by the other's feet. You can lie all the way down or hold yourselves up on your elbows and forearms. The receiver wraps their legs around the giver—one leg under the giver and one leg over their waist.

 WHAT'S GOOD ABOUT IT

You each have a free hand to use as you please. Maybe for some thigh massage, ass, and/or ball play. Your hands, your choice.

 MAKE IT BETTER

Try kissing and sucking each other's toes for a next-level, ultra-connected feel.

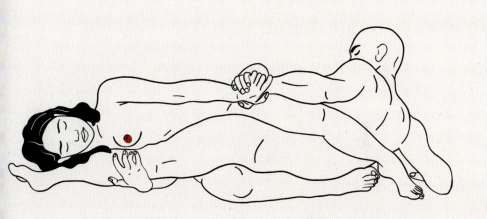

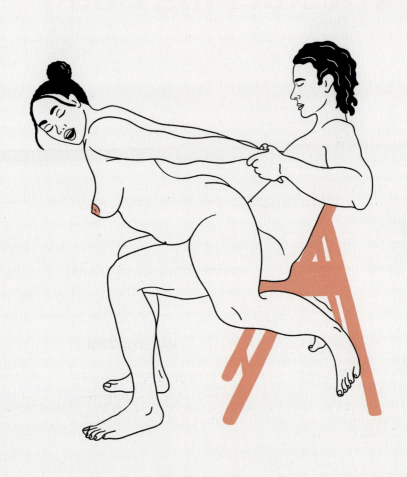

ADVANCED MODE

The Rocking Chair
ROCK YOUR WORLDS.

HOW TO DO IT

The giver sits in a chair and the receiver straddles their partner's lap, facing away. Grab each other's hands, then the receiver leans forward so that their chest is over their partner's legs. The receiver can let their legs dangle or wrap them around the back of the chair for more stability.

WHAT'S GOOD ABOUT IT

You can adjust the type of motion depending on what you like. The giver can pull their partner by their arms for a gentle rocking movement or thrust up with their hips for more intensity.

MAKE IT BETTER

Try it in an actual rocking chair and let the chair guide some of the motions.

Forbidden Yoga
TURN THAT SEX UPSIDE DOWN.

HOW TO DO IT

The receiver lies on the floor. The giver stands with both feet on either side of their partner's head, holds onto their partner's legs, and lifts them up to press them onto their penis or strap-on. The receiver bends their knees to give their partner something to grasp onto and hold themselves up in a shoulder stand from yoga.

WHAT'S GOOD ABOUT IT

Trying something challenging and new forces both people to really focus on what's happening. That kind of focus leads to more mindful and intense sex.

MAKE IT BETTER

Make this a nonpenetrative position by having the giver kneel on the ground, spread their partner's legs, and give the receiver oral.

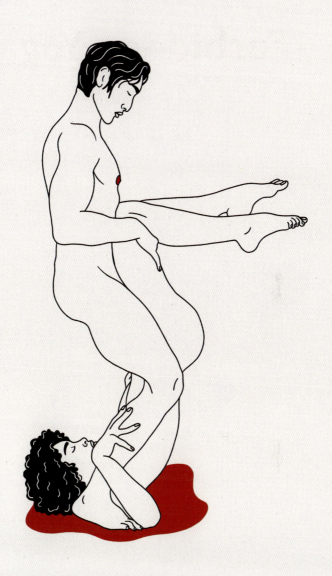

ADVANCED MODE

The Starter Gun
ON YOUR MARK.

HOW TO DO IT

The giver sits on an ottoman, with their hips at the edge and their hands behind them, resting on the floor. The receiver faces away from their partner and bends down, crouching down on their feet and hands, with their knees bent and arms straight.

WHAT'S GOOD ABOUT IT

Whether used as an anal or vaginal position, this allows the giver a great view of their penis or strap-on sliding in and out of their partner.

MAKE IT BETTER

This position lends itself to dominance and submission play. Have the giver instruct the receiver how they would like them to move (e.g., "Slowly, like you mean it" or "Moan for me.").

Quarto.com

© 2025 Quarto Publishing Group USA Inc.

First Published in 2025 by Fair Winds Press, an imprint of The Quarto Group, 100 Cummings Center, Suite 265-D, Beverly, MA 01915, USA.
T (978) 282-9590 F (978) 283-2742

All rights reserved. No part of this book may be reproduced in any form without written permission of the copyright owners. All images in this book have been reproduced with the knowledge and prior consent of the artists concerned, and no responsibility is accepted by producer, publisher, or printer for any infringement of copyright or otherwise, arising from the contents of this publication. Every effort has been made to ensure that credits accurately comply with information supplied. We apologize for any inaccuracies that may have occurred and will resolve inaccurate or missing information in a subsequent reprinting of the book.

Fair Winds Press titles are also available at discount for retail, wholesale, promotional, and bulk purchase. For details, contact the Special Sales Manager by email at specialsales@quarto.com or by mail at The Quarto Group, Attn: Special Sales Manager, 100 Cummings Center, Suite 265-D, Beverly, MA 01915, USA.

29 28 27 26 25   1 2 3 4 5

ISBN: 978-0-7603-9655-1

Digital edition published in 2025
eISBN: 978-0-7603-9656-8

Library of Congress Cataloging-in-Publication Data is available.

Design and Page Layout: Studio Quarante Douze Inc
Illustration: Clémence Langevin, clemencelangevin.com

Printed in Hong Kong

The information in this book is for educational purposes only.
Any type of sexual activity should be consensual.